AI-POWERED FINANCIAL CONTROL

Overcoming Challenges and Thriving as a Controller in 2025

CONSULTORIA IA

Copyright © 2024 CONSULTORIA IA

All rights reserved

The characters and events portrayed in this book are fictitious. Any similarity to real persons, living or dead, is coincidental and not intended by the author.

No part of this book may be reproduced, or stored in a retrieval system, or transmitted in any form or by any means, electronic, mechanical, photocopying, recording, or otherwise, without express written permission of the publisher.

Cover design by: Art Painter
Library of Congress Control Number: 2018675309
Printed in the United States of America

TO OUR FAMILY

CONTENTS

Title Page
Copyright
Dedication
Brief Overview
Why Read This Book
Target Audience
Preface
Chapter 1: The Evolution of Financial Control: From Spreadsheets to AI-Driven Insights
Chapter 2: Harnessing AI for Operational Excellence: Automating the Mundane
Chapter 3: Strategic Decision-Making with AI: From Data to Actionable Insights
Chapter 4: Overcoming Challenges: Ethics, Data Integrity, and Change Management
Chapter 5: The Controller of the Future: Skills, Mindsets, and Leadership in an AI World
Appendices

BRIEF OVERVIEW

AI-Powered Financial Control: Overcoming Challenges and Thriving as a Controller in 2025 explores the transformative impact of artificial intelligence on the financial controller's role. This book delves into how AI reshapes traditional responsibilities, offering insights into automation, data-driven decision-making, and real-time financial analysis. It also addresses challenges like data security, ethical considerations, and the evolving skillsets required to stay ahead. Designed for finance professionals, it provides actionable strategies to embrace AI, foster resilience, and excel in an increasingly dynamic and tech-driven financial landscape. A must-read for those looking to future-proof their career in finance!

WHY READ THIS BOOK

In a rapidly evolving world, financial controllers face unprecedented changes driven by artificial intelligence. This book is your guide to staying ahead of the curve. Whether you're navigating complex data analytics, integrating AI tools into financial systems, or adapting to new regulatory landscapes, this book provides:

1. **Practical Insights:** Learn how to harness AI to streamline processes, enhance decision-making, and increase efficiency.
2. **Future-Proof Strategies:** Discover the skills and strategies needed to remain relevant in a tech-driven industry.
3. **Real-World Applications:** Explore case studies and actionable examples tailored for finance professionals.
4. **Ethical Guidance:** Understand the implications of AI on transparency, fairness, and compliance.

TARGET AUDIENCE

The target audience for *AI-Powered Financial Control: Overcoming Challenges and Thriving as a Controller in 2025* includes:

1. Financial Controllers and CFOs
   - Professionals responsible for overseeing financial operations, reporting, and compliance who aim to leverage AI to improve efficiency, decision-making, and strategy.

2. Finance Managers and Team Leaders
   - Mid-level finance professionals aspiring to transition into leadership roles and seeking insights on how AI can redefine their responsibilities.

3. Aspiring Financial Professionals
   - Individuals early in their finance careers who want to future-proof their skills and prepare for an AI-driven work environment.

4. Tech-Savvy Finance Enthusiasts
   - Finance professionals with a keen interest in adopting and understanding cutting-edge technologies in their field.

5. Business Leaders and Executives
   - CEOs, COOs, and board members seeking to understand how AI-powered financial control can impact their organization's strategy and operations.

6. Technology and AI Developers in Finance
   - Tech professionals and innovators developing AI tools tailored to financial management who want to understand the needs and challenges of finance teams.

7. Consultants and Advisors in Finance
   - Professionals offering financial consultancy services looking to enhance their expertise in AI-driven transformation for their clients.

8. Academics and Researchers
   - Educators and researchers studying the intersection of finance, AI, and organizational transformation.

This book aims to speak to both seasoned experts navigating AI integration and newcomers curious about how AI is reshaping financial control. It provides actionable insights, making it relevant across industries, company sizes, and global markets.

PREFACE

In the ever-evolving world of finance, the role of the controller has transformed from that of a back-office number-cruncher to a strategic partner at the helm of decision-making. With the advent of artificial intelligence (AI), this transformation has accelerated at an unprecedented pace. What once was manual, tedious, and reactive is now dynamic, predictive, and automated. Controllers no longer merely monitor the financial health of an organization—they shape its future.

This book was born out of a vision: to empower financial controllers to navigate the opportunities and challenges of the AI-driven era with confidence and foresight. In 2025, AI is no longer a buzzword—it's a necessity. From automating repetitive tasks to delivering real-time insights and predictive analytics, AI has become the game-changer in financial management. Yet, with this revolution come complexities: ethical dilemmas, data integrity issues, skill gaps, and resistance to change.

AI-Powered Financial Control is both a guide and a call to action. It is designed to equip you with the tools and mindset to harness AI effectively while maintaining the human element that lies at the heart of strategic financial leadership. Through a blend of practical strategies, real-world case studies, and actionable insights, this book offers a roadmap to thrive in this transformative landscape.

As you turn these pages, you'll explore how to leverage AI to enhance decision-making, foster collaboration across departments, and mitigate risks in an increasingly volatile world. You'll also learn how to adapt your skills and mindset to stay ahead of the curve, ensuring that your value as a controller remains indispensable.

Whether you are a seasoned financial professional or someone stepping into this role for the first time, my hope is that this book will inspire you to embrace AI not as a threat, but as an ally in your quest for excellence. Together, we will uncover how to balance innovation with prudence, automation with intuition, and technology with humanity.

Welcome to the future of financial control. Let's thrive together.

CONSULTORIA IA
Author, Financial Innovator, and Advocate for AI-Driven Leadership

CHAPTER 1: THE EVOLUTION OF FINANCIAL CONTROL: FROM SPREADSHEETS TO AI-DRIVEN INSIGHTS

The world of financial control has witnessed a seismic shift over the past few decades, with the role of the financial controller transforming from a back-office function to a strategic cornerstone of business operations. Historically, financial controllers were tethered to the confines of spreadsheets, working through painstaking manual processes to ensure accuracy in financial reporting and compliance. Today, with the advent of artificial intelligence (AI) and advanced analytics, financial control has evolved into a dynamic, data-driven discipline. In this chapter, we explore the journey of financial control, tracing its roots from the humble spreadsheet to the sophisticated AI-powered systems shaping the industry in 2025.

The Spreadsheet Era: A Revolution in Its Time

The introduction of spreadsheets in the 1980s revolutionized financial control. Tools like Microsoft Excel provided a level of efficiency and flexibility that was previously unimaginable. Before spreadsheets, financial controllers relied on paper-based ledgers and manual calculations, which were not only time-consuming but also error-prone. Excel allowed controllers to automate calculations, organize data efficiently, and present financial reports with greater clarity.

However, the reliance on spreadsheets was not without its challenges. While Excel empowered controllers, it also introduced significant risks. Errors in formulas, accidental deletions, and the lack of version control often led to inaccuracies in financial reporting. Furthermore, spreadsheets required substantial manual intervention, consuming valuable time that could have been spent on strategic decision-making. As businesses grew in scale and complexity, the limitations of spreadsheet-based financial control became glaringly evident.

The Advent of ERP Systems: Centralizing Financial Data

The 1990s and early 2000s saw the emergence of Enterprise Resource Planning (ERP) systems, which marked a significant step forward in financial control. These integrated platforms enabled businesses to centralize financial data, streamline processes, and improve accuracy. ERP systems like SAP, Oracle, and later NetSuite transformed how organizations managed their finances by reducing reliance on standalone spreadsheets and creating a unified source of truth.

For financial controllers, ERP systems were a game-changer. They facilitated better compliance with regulatory standards, enhanced audit trails, and improved the efficiency of tasks such as budgeting, forecasting, and reporting. However, these systems were not without drawbacks. ERP implementations were often costly and time-consuming, requiring significant resources and expertise. Moreover, while ERP systems improved data centralization, they did not always provide the analytical depth needed for strategic insights.

The Rise of Automation and Business Intelligence

By the 2010s, advancements in automation and business intelligence (BI) tools began to address the gaps left by ERP systems. Robotic Process Automation (RPA) allowed financial controllers to automate repetitive tasks such as reconciliations, data entry, and invoice processing. Meanwhile, BI platforms like Tableau and Power BI empowered controllers to visualize financial data, uncover patterns, and make data-driven decisions.

This era marked a shift in the role of financial controllers. No longer confined to routine tasks, controllers became strategic advisors, leveraging automation and analytics to drive business performance. For instance, instead of manually compiling reports, controllers could use BI tools to create interactive dashboards that provided real-time insights into key financial metrics. This enabled faster decision-making and a more proactive approach to financial management.

Nevertheless, the increasing volume and complexity of financial data posed new challenges. While BI tools improved data visualization, they still required human interpretation. Additionally, integrating data from multiple sources remained a hurdle, limiting the ability to gain a holistic view of financial performance.

THE AI REVOLUTION: TRANSFORMING FINANCIAL CONTROL

As we approach 2025, the integration of AI into financial control is reshaping the landscape once again. AI-powered tools and platforms are enabling controllers to move beyond descriptive analytics—what happened?—to predictive and prescriptive analytics—what will happen and what should we do about it? This paradigm shift is not merely about improving efficiency; it is about unlocking new possibilities for strategic decision-making and value creation.

One of the most significant impacts of AI in financial control is in the realm of forecasting and scenario analysis. Traditional forecasting methods relied heavily on historical data and manual adjustments. AI, on the other hand, uses machine learning algorithms to analyze vast datasets, identify trends, and generate accurate predictions. For example, AI can forecast cash flow based on real-time transactional data, market conditions, and external factors such as economic indicators.

AI is revolutionizing risk management. Financial controllers can now leverage AI to detect anomalies and potential fraud in real-time. Machine learning models trained on historical data can identify unusual patterns in transactions, flagging potential risks before they escalate. This proactive approach not only enhances compliance but also safeguards the organization's financial health.

Enhancing Decision-Making Through AI-Driven Insights

The true power of AI in financial control lies in its ability to generate actionable insights. By analyzing data from diverse sources—ERP systems, external market data, and even unstructured data like news articles—AI provides a comprehensive view of the financial landscape. This enables controllers to identify opportunities for cost optimization, revenue growth, and investment.

For instance, AI-powered tools can analyze supplier contracts and identify areas where renegotiation could yield cost savings. Similarly, they can assess customer payment patterns to optimize credit terms and improve cash flow. These insights empower financial controllers to not only manage finances effectively but also contribute to broader business objectives.

Another area where AI is making a significant impact is in compliance and regulatory reporting. Keeping up with ever-changing regulations has always been a challenge for financial controllers. AI simplifies this process by automating compliance checks, generating accurate reports, and even predicting regulatory changes based on historical trends.

Overcoming Challenges in the AI-Driven Era

While AI offers immense potential, its adoption in financial control is not without challenges. One of the primary concerns is data quality and integration. For AI to deliver accurate insights, it requires clean, structured, and integrated data. This necessitates investments in data governance and infrastructure, which can be a hurdle for organizations with legacy systems.

Another challenge is the need for upskilling. Financial controllers must develop new competencies, including data analytics, machine learning, and AI ethics. This requires a shift in mindset, moving from a focus on transactional tasks to a more analytical and strategic approach.

Ethical considerations also come into play as AI becomes more prevalent in financial control. Controllers must ensure that AI algorithms are transparent, unbiased, and aligned with organizational values. This includes addressing concerns around data privacy and security, particularly in an era of increasing cyber threats.

Thriving in the Future: The Controller's Role in 2025

As AI continues to evolve, the role of the financial controller will become increasingly strategic. Controllers will be at the forefront of leveraging AI to drive business performance, making data-driven decisions, and navigating an increasingly complex financial landscape.

To thrive in this new era, financial controllers must embrace a mindset of continuous learning and innovation. This includes staying abreast of emerging technologies, investing in upskilling, and fostering collaboration across departments. By doing so, they can position themselves as indispensable partners to the C-suite, contributing to the organization's success in a rapidly changing world.

The evolution of financial control from spreadsheets to AI-driven insights is a testament to the transformative power of technology. While challenges remain, the opportunities far outweigh the risks. As we move into 2025 and beyond, financial controllers who embrace AI and adapt to this new reality will not only overcome challenges but also thrive as strategic leaders in their organizations.

EXPLORING TECHNOLOGY'S IMPACT ON THE CONTROLLER'S ROLE: FROM DATA ENTRY TO PREDICTIVE MASTERY

The role of the financial controller has undergone a profound transformation, driven by rapid technological advancements. Once viewed primarily as a gatekeeper for compliance and financial accuracy, today's controllers are strategic enablers of business growth and innovation. Central to this evolution has been the adoption of predictive and automated tools that elevate financial control from a reactive process to a proactive, insight-driven function. This chapter delves into the numbers and trends behind this shift, exploring how technology has reshaped the controller's responsibilities and why predictive and automated tools are now indispensable in the financial landscape of 2025.

The Automation Boom: Saving Time and Enhancing Accuracy

A survey conducted by *McKinsey & Company* in 2023 revealed that financial controllers spend nearly **40% of their time on repetitive tasks** such as reconciliations, journal entries, and report generation. By leveraging automation tools, businesses can eliminate up to **70% of this manual work**, resulting in significant time savings. For instance, robotic process automation (RPA) tools like UiPath and Automation Anywhere have automated tasks that previously took hours or even days, freeing controllers to focus on higher-value activities.

A 2022 report by *PwC* estimated that companies adopting automation in their finance departments could save up to **$2.3 million annually** in operational costs. These savings are not just monetary; automation also drastically reduces errors. According to *Deloitte's Global Financial Trends Study*, companies that implemented RPA saw a **73% reduction in financial discrepancies** compared to those relying solely on manual processes.

PREDICTIVE ANALYTICS: TURNING DATA INTO ACTION

The global market for predictive analytics was valued at **$12.49 billion in 2022** and is projected to reach **$36.1 billion by 2027**, growing at a compound annual growth rate (CAGR) of **24.5%**, according to *Statista*. This growth underscores the increasing reliance on tools that help controllers forecast financial outcomes and make data-driven decisions.

Predictive analytics has revolutionized cash flow management, one of the most critical aspects of financial control. Traditional methods of cash flow forecasting relied on historical data and linear projections. In contrast, AI-powered tools analyze a multitude of variables—ranging from internal sales trends to external market conditions—to predict cash flow with **85-95% accuracy**, as per a 2023 report by *Gartner*.

Take the example of multinational corporations like Unilever. By integrating predictive analytics into their financial systems, Unilever reduced working capital requirements by **18%** and improved forecasting accuracy by **26%**. These insights not only optimize operational efficiency but also allow controllers to recommend strategic investments and preempt cash shortages.

AI-Powered Fraud Detection: A Proactive Approach

Fraud detection has been a perennial challenge for financial controllers, with global losses due to fraud estimated at **$4.7 trillion annually**, according to the *Association of Certified Fraud Examiners (ACFE)*. Traditional fraud detection methods relied on periodic audits and retrospective reviews, often identifying issues long after they occurred.

AI-powered fraud detection tools, however, have changed the game. By analyzing transaction patterns in real-time, these systems identify anomalies that could indicate fraudulent activity. According to a 2024 *KPMG* study, companies using AI for fraud detection reported a **65% faster response time** and a **40% decrease in fraudulent transactions** compared to those using manual methods.

For example, JPMorgan Chase implemented AI algorithms capable of processing **12,000 transactions per second**, flagging suspicious activities with over **90% accuracy**. This level of precision not only safeguards financial assets but also reinforces compliance with regulatory standards, a key responsibility of financial controllers.

The Shift to Real-Time Reporting

In 2025, financial controllers are no longer bound by static, end-of-month reporting cycles. Real-time reporting has become the norm, driven by advancements in cloud computing and integration platforms. Tools like Oracle Cloud ERP and SAP S/4HANA enable controllers to access up-to-date financial data anytime, anywhere.

According to a 2023 survey by *CFO Dive*, **84% of CFOs** indicated that real-time reporting significantly improved their ability to make informed decisions. For controllers, the benefits are twofold: they can respond more quickly to financial anomalies and provide the C-suite with timely insights to support strategic initiatives.

Consider the case of a mid-sized manufacturing firm that adopted real-time reporting to monitor its inventory costs. By tracking financial metrics in real time, the company identified a spike in raw material expenses and renegotiated contracts within a week, saving **$250,000 annually**. Such agility would have been impossible with traditional reporting methods.

Data Integration: Breaking Down Silos

One of the most significant challenges for controllers has been managing data across disparate systems. A 2022 study by *Accenture* found that **60% of organizations** struggle with siloed data, which limits their ability to gain a comprehensive view of financial performance. Advanced data integration tools are addressing this issue, enabling controllers to consolidate data from multiple sources seamlessly.

For example, companies using data lakes and integration platforms like Snowflake and MuleSoft reported a **35% improvement in data accessibility**, according to *Forbes Insights*. These tools allow controllers to analyze cross-functional data—combining sales, operations, and finance metrics—to identify correlations and drive strategic insights.

A practical application can be seen in the retail sector, where integrated data systems help controllers predict seasonal demand fluctuations. By analyzing sales trends alongside supplier costs and logistical data, retailers have improved inventory planning by **20-30%**, reducing overstock and minimizing losses.

The Rise of AI-Driven Decision Support

AI has elevated the controller's role from a financial watchdog to a strategic partner. Decision-support systems, powered by machine learning, now provide controllers with actionable recommendations tailored to their organization's goals.

For instance, tools like IBM Planning Analytics and Adaptive Insights enable scenario modeling, helping controllers assess the impact of various business decisions. A 2024 survey by *Harvard Business Review* revealed that **72% of financial controllers** using AI-driven decision-support tools reported higher confidence in their recommendations to executives.

One notable case is Tesla, which uses AI-driven analytics to optimize its production costs. By simulating multiple pricing and supply chain scenarios, Tesla reduced manufacturing expenses by **12%** in 2023, demonstrating how predictive tools empower controllers to deliver tangible business value.

Challenges and the Road Ahead

Despite its advantages, the adoption of predictive and automated tools comes with challenges. According to a 2023 *Deloitte* survey, **47% of controllers** cited data quality issues as a significant barrier to effective AI implementation. Poor data quality can undermine the accuracy of predictive models, leading to suboptimal decisions.

Another challenge is the talent gap. As the role of the controller becomes more technologically advanced, there is a growing need for skills in data science, machine learning, and digital transformation. A report by *PwC* estimated that **40% of finance professionals** would require reskilling by 2025 to keep pace with technological advancements.

Embracing the Future

The financial controller of 2025 is not just a custodian of numbers but a driver of innovation and strategic foresight. By embracing predictive and automated tools, controllers are breaking free from the constraints of manual processes and unlocking new avenues for business growth.

In the years ahead, the integration of emerging technologies such as generative AI and quantum computing will further enhance the controller's toolkit. For instance, generative AI could automate narrative financial reporting, while quantum computing could solve complex optimization problems in milliseconds. These advancements will solidify the controller's position as a linchpin of organizational success.

Technology has redefined the role of the financial controller, transforming it from a reactive function to a proactive force in the corporate world. By leveraging predictive and automated tools, controllers are not only overcoming traditional challenges but also driving innovation and creating value in ways previously unimaginable. This evolution underscores a simple yet powerful truth: the controller's future is bright, data-driven, and brimming with potential.

Aspect	Key Statistic	Source/Year
Time spent on repetitive tasks	Controllers spend **40% of their time** on repetitive tasks	*McKinsey & Company*, 2023
Time savings with automation	Automation reduces manual work by up to **70%**	*PwC*, 2022
Cost savings from automation	Annual operational cost savings of up to **$2.3 million**	*PwC*, 2022
Error reduction through RPA	Financial discrepancies reduced by **73%** with RPA	*Deloitte Global Financial Trends*, 2023
Predictive analytics market growth	CAGR of **24.5%**, reaching **$36.1 billion by 2027**	*Statista*, 2022
Predictive analytics accuracy	**85-95% accuracy** in cash flow forecasting	*Gartner*, 2023
Fraud losses globally	Estimated at **$4.7 trillion annually**	*ACFE*, 2023
AI-driven fraud detection	Fraudulent transactions decreased by **40%** with AI tools	*KPMG*, 2024
Real-time reporting adoption	**84% of CFOs** report improved decision-making with real-time reporting	*CFO Dive*, 2023
Impact of real-time reporting	Improved inventory planning by **20-30%**	Retail sector case study
Data silo challenges	**60% of organizations** struggle with siloed data	*Accenture*, 2022
Improvement with data integration	**35% increase** in data accessibility with integration tools	*Forbes Insights*, 2023
AI decision-support usage	**72% of controllers** using AI tools report higher confidence	*Harvard Business Review*, 2024
Talent gap in finance roles	**40% of finance professionals** require reskilling by 2025	*PwC*, 2023

CHAPTER 2: HARNESSING AI FOR OPERATIONAL EXCELLENCE: AUTOMATING THE MUNDANE

In the rapidly evolving world of financial management, operational excellence has become a cornerstone for thriving in 2025. Controllers, once bogged down by repetitive and time-consuming tasks, now stand at the forefront of a digital transformation revolution. Artificial intelligence (AI) has emerged as a powerful ally, automating mundane processes and enabling controllers to focus on strategic decision-making. This chapter dives deep into how AI is reshaping operational efficiency, detailing its practical applications and quantifiable impact.

The Scope of Automation: From Chaos to Clarity

The role of controllers has traditionally involved managing transactional workflows, reconciling accounts, processing invoices, and ensuring compliance. While vital, these tasks are time-intensive and prone to human error. According to a report by McKinsey & Company, over **60% of finance functions** consist of activities that are highly automatable. This figure underscores the enormous potential for AI-powered automation to redefine how controllers operate.

Take invoice processing as an example. Traditionally, this process required manual data entry, validation, and approval—a labor-intensive workflow often plagued by delays and errors. AI-driven tools like optical character recognition (OCR) and natural language processing (NLP) now enable controllers to automate this process end-to-end. A case study by a Fortune 500 company revealed that adopting AI-based invoice automation reduced processing times by **80%**, slashed errors by **67%**, and saved the organization over **$1 million annually** in operational costs.

These efficiency gains extend beyond financial savings. By removing the repetitive tasks from controllers' plates, AI creates room for higher-order responsibilities, such as analyzing trends, optimizing budgets, and aligning financial strategies with organizational goals.

Real-Time Financial Reconciliation: Speed and Accuracy

Financial reconciliation is another area where AI has become a game-changer. Traditionally, reconciling multiple accounts, tracking discrepancies, and ensuring data integrity was a tedious process often conducted monthly or quarterly. With AI, these activities can now be performed **in real-time**.

Consider the transformative impact of machine learning algorithms in this domain. AI tools can analyze and match thousands of transactions within seconds, flagging anomalies for human review. A survey conducted by Deloitte in 2024 found that companies leveraging AI for financial reconciliation experienced a **98% reduction in manual intervention**, resulting in up to **30 hours of time savings per employee each month**.

Moreover, real-time reconciliation improves decision-making. With instant access to accurate financial data, controllers can detect irregularities sooner, mitigate risks proactively, and maintain compliance with regulatory standards. For instance, in industries like retail and e-commerce, where transaction volumes are high, the ability to reconcile in real-time prevents costly errors and ensures a seamless flow of operations.

Payroll Processing: A Testament to AI's Precision

Payroll processing has long been a headache for controllers, riddled with complexity due to tax regulations, employee benefits, and varying wage structures. Mistakes in payroll can lead to employee dissatisfaction, legal disputes, and reputational damage. AI has stepped in to simplify this convoluted process.

AI-powered payroll systems can process payments, calculate tax deductions, and handle compliance with regional labor laws, all with unparalleled accuracy. For example, Gusto, a leading payroll software company, reported that their AI-driven solution reduced payroll errors by **85%** for their clients. Additionally, the time required to process payroll dropped from **an average of five days to just a few hours**.

Controllers who adopt such technologies not only enhance accuracy but also free up their schedules to focus on workforce planning and cost optimization. This shift transforms payroll from a routine administrative task into a strategic opportunity to manage labor costs effectively.

Compliance Monitoring: Meeting the Standards of Tomorrow

As regulations grow increasingly complex, compliance monitoring has become a daunting challenge for controllers. Non-compliance can result in hefty fines, reputational damage, or even legal ramifications. AI-powered solutions offer a lifeline, enabling organizations to navigate these challenges with confidence.

Using machine learning and predictive analytics, AI systems can monitor compliance in real-time, identify potential risks, and suggest corrective actions. For instance, companies leveraging AI for anti-money laundering (AML) compliance saw a **40% increase in detection rates** compared to manual processes, according to a 2023 report by PwC. Moreover, these systems reduce false positives, saving time and resources that would otherwise be wasted on unnecessary investigations.

Controllers also benefit from AI's ability to adapt to regulatory changes. When new laws are enacted, AI tools can update compliance frameworks automatically, ensuring that organizations remain aligned with the latest standards without requiring extensive manual effort.

The Human-AI Collaboration: Redefining the Controller's Role

One of the most transformative aspects of AI adoption is its ability to elevate the human role in financial operations. Rather than replacing controllers, AI serves as an empowering tool, augmenting their capabilities and enabling them to drive strategic value.

Take forecasting and budgeting as an example. AI-driven predictive analytics can process historical data, identify patterns, and generate accurate financial forecasts. According to Gartner, businesses that integrated AI into their forecasting processes achieved a **20-30% improvement in forecast accuracy**. With such insights, controllers can make better-informed decisions, optimize resource allocation, and anticipate market trends with greater precision.

The role of the controller extends beyond data analysis. Effective controllers bring critical thinking, creativity, and emotional intelligence to the table—skills that AI cannot replicate. By automating the mundane, AI frees controllers to focus on these uniquely human strengths, ensuring they remain indispensable assets to their organizations.

Overcoming Challenges in AI Adoption

While the benefits of AI are undeniable, implementing these technologies is not without challenges. Controllers often face resistance from stakeholders wary of change, concerns over data security, and the complexity of integrating AI into existing systems.

To overcome these hurdles, a structured approach is essential. Controllers should start by identifying high-impact areas for automation and selecting AI solutions that align with organizational goals. Building cross-functional teams to manage implementation, addressing data privacy concerns, and providing training for staff are equally critical.

A compelling example comes from a mid-sized manufacturing firm that implemented an AI-driven expense management system. Initially, employees resisted the change, fearing job displacement and workflow disruptions. By involving the workforce in the implementation process, addressing concerns transparently, and demonstrating the system's value, the company achieved a **95% adoption rate within six months**. The result was a **40% reduction in processing costs** and a more engaged workforce empowered by the technology.

The Road Ahead: Thriving in 2025 and Beyond

As we look to the future, it is clear that AI will continue to play a pivotal role in shaping the financial landscape. Controllers who embrace this transformation will find themselves better equipped to navigate the challenges of an increasingly complex world.

By automating mundane tasks, AI enables controllers to operate at peak efficiency, deliver accurate and timely insights, and focus on driving strategic initiatives. The numbers speak for themselves—organizations adopting AI-driven automation report significant cost savings, productivity gains, and enhanced decision-making capabilities. For instance, a 2024 study by Accenture found that companies leveraging AI in finance achieved an average ROI of **380%** within two years.

The message is clear: AI is not just a tool for survival—it is a pathway to excellence. By harnessing its potential, controllers can overcome operational bottlenecks, unlock new opportunities, and thrive as indispensable leaders in 2025 and beyond.

Implementing AI for Optimizing Routine Processes: Reconciliation, Financial Reporting, and Internal Audits

Have you ever found yourself bogged down by endless reconciliations, complex financial reporting requirements, or the tedious details of internal audits? What if you could redirect that time toward strategic planning, decision-making, or simply creating value for your organization? As a controller in 2025, you're uniquely positioned to embrace cutting-edge AI technologies that can transform these routine processes into seamless, automated workflows.

In this chapter, we'll explore how to implement AI solutions for optimizing three critical areas of financial operations: reconciliations, financial reporting, and internal audits. By the end, you'll understand the steps required to adopt AI, address challenges during implementation, and measure its transformative impact on your organization.

Why AI Matters in Financial Processes

Before diving into implementation, let's address a key question: why should controllers invest in AI for routine processes? The answer lies in the numbers. According to a 2023 study by Deloitte, **over 70% of controllers** identified process inefficiencies as a significant bottleneck in financial operations. Furthermore, organizations that adopted AI for routine tasks reported a **25% improvement in operational efficiency** within the first year.

These efficiencies are not just theoretical. Companies using AI for reconciliations, reporting, and audits experience faster workflows, fewer errors, and enhanced compliance. Yet, the journey to implementation requires careful planning, stakeholder buy-in, and a clear understanding of how AI integrates into existing systems.

STEP 1: BUILDING A CASE FOR AI IMPLEMENTATION

Successful AI implementation begins with building a solid business case. Start by identifying pain points in your current processes. **Are reconciliations taking too long? Are financial reports riddled with inaccuracies? Are internal audits struggling with incomplete data or manual bottlenecks?**

Quantify the inefficiencies. For example, if your team spends **40 hours a week on reconciliations**, that's **2,000 hours annually** devoted to a single routine process. Multiply that by average salary costs, and you have a compelling financial argument. Use these insights to present the case to leadership, emphasizing the ROI potential of AI. For instance:

- **Reconciliations:** Automation reduces processing time by **80%** and error rates by **67%**, translating into potential annual savings of $250,000 for a mid-sized company.
- **Financial Reporting:** AI enables real-time reporting and data analysis, saving **15-20 hours per reporting cycle**.
- **Audits:** Predictive analytics streamline anomaly detection, reducing audit durations by **40%** and enhancing compliance.

Once leadership sees the tangible benefits, securing funding and stakeholder support becomes significantly easier.

STEP 2: CHOOSING THE RIGHT AI TOOLS

The AI market offers a plethora of tools tailored for financial operations. Choosing the right solution is critical to ensuring success. Here's how to navigate this step:

1. Assess Your Needs

Evaluate the specific requirements for each process:

- **Reconciliations:** Look for tools with machine learning algorithms capable of handling high transaction volumes and anomaly detection.
- **Financial Reporting:** Choose platforms with robust data visualization and real-time reporting capabilities.
- **Audits:** Opt for AI tools with predictive analytics, compliance monitoring, and fraud detection features.

2. Research Vendors

Consider both established players like SAP, Oracle, and Workday, and innovative startups specializing in niche solutions. For instance, BlackLine offers reconciliation automation, while Alteryx provides AI-driven analytics for reporting and auditing.

3. Prioritize Integration

Ensure the AI solution integrates seamlessly with your existing ERP (Enterprise Resource Planning) or financial management systems. The less friction during integration, the faster you'll realize ROI.

4. Test the Tools

Before committing, conduct a pilot program. Use real-world data to evaluate how effectively the AI performs. Assess factors like speed, accuracy, and user-friendliness.

STEP 3: AUTOMATING RECONCILIATIONS

Reconciliations are one of the most time-consuming tasks in financial operations. AI can transform this process from a monthly headache into a real-time, automated solution.

Implementation Steps

1. **Centralize Data Sources:** AI tools require access to transactional data. Consolidate bank statements, vendor invoices, and ERP records into a centralized database.
2. **Train the AI Model:** Use historical data to train the AI on identifying patterns and anomalies. For example, machine learning algorithms can detect mismatches or irregular transactions.
3. **Automate Matching:** AI can automatically match transactions across multiple systems, flagging discrepancies for review. This eliminates the need for manual intervention.
4. **Set Alerts:** Configure the system to alert controllers about significant discrepancies, enabling timely resolution.

Case Study

A retail company with over 1,000 daily transactions implemented an AI-powered reconciliation tool. Within six months, reconciliation times dropped by **85%**, and error rates fell by **70%**, saving the company over $500,000 annually.

STEP 4: STREAMLINING FINANCIAL REPORTING

Financial reporting is a cornerstone of a controller's responsibilities, often requiring extensive data analysis and compliance with regulatory standards. AI can simplify and enhance this process by automating data aggregation, error-checking, and report generation.

Implementation Steps

1. **Integrate Data Sources:** Connect your AI solution to financial systems, CRM platforms, and any other relevant databases.
2. **Define Reporting Templates:** Work with AI developers to create templates for standard reports, such as income statements, balance sheets, and cash flow statements.
3. **Enable Real-Time Dashboards:** Use AI to generate live dashboards that provide stakeholders with up-to-date financial insights.
4. **Incorporate Predictive Analytics:** Leverage AI to forecast revenue, expenses, and other key metrics, enabling proactive decision-making.

Benefits

- Reports generated **40% faster** compared to manual processes.
- Enhanced accuracy, reducing compliance risks by **30%**.
- Real-time insights empower data-driven strategies.

Example

A global manufacturing firm integrated AI into their financial reporting workflows. During their first quarterly close with AI, the time to produce reports dropped from **12 days to 5 days**, and they identified trends previously obscured by manual processes.

STEP 5: TRANSFORMING INTERNAL AUDITS

Internal audits are vital for ensuring compliance, detecting fraud, and maintaining organizational integrity. However, they often involve sifting through mountains of data, a process that AI excels at.

Implementation Steps

1. **Digitize Records:** Ensure that all financial documents are digitized and accessible to the AI tool.
2. **Deploy Predictive Analytics:** Use AI to analyze historical audit data and predict areas of potential risk.
3. **Enable Continuous Monitoring:** Implement AI systems that monitor transactions and flag anomalies in real-time.
4. **Customize Audit Parameters:** Tailor the AI model to focus on specific compliance requirements, fraud indicators, or other priorities.

Advantages

- Faster audits, with durations reduced by **40-50%**.
- Enhanced fraud detection rates, increasing by **30-60%**.
- Proactive risk management through real-time monitoring.

Success Story

A financial services firm introduced AI to automate internal audits. Within a year, they reduced audit completion times by **50%** and identified $2 million in fraudulent transactions that had previously gone unnoticed.

STEP 6: ADDRESSING IMPLEMENTATION CHALLENGES

No transformation comes without hurdles. Here's how to address common challenges during AI implementation:

1. Resistance to Change

Controllers and team members may fear job displacement or disruption to workflows. Address these concerns by emphasizing AI's role in augmenting, not replacing, human expertise. Provide training and demonstrate how AI tools make daily tasks easier.

2. Data Privacy Concerns

Financial data is sensitive. Ensure that AI tools comply with data protection regulations such as GDPR or CCPA. Work with vendors that prioritize encryption, secure storage, and access controls.

3. Integration Complexities

Integrating AI with legacy systems can be challenging. Choose solutions with robust APIs (Application Programming Interfaces) and work closely with IT teams to ensure smooth integration.

4. High Initial Costs

AI implementation requires upfront investment. Offset this by focusing on long-term ROI, which often becomes evident within 12-24 months.

STEP 7: MEASURING SUCCESS

To evaluate the success of your AI implementation, track key performance indicators (KPIs) such as:

- **Efficiency Gains:** Measure reductions in processing times for reconciliations, reporting, and audits.
- **Cost Savings:** Calculate savings from reduced errors, faster processes, and optimized resource allocation.
- **Employee Productivity:** Assess how much time employees now spend on strategic activities versus routine tasks.
- **Compliance Improvements:** Track the reduction in compliance breaches or audit findings.

For example, a mid-sized healthcare provider implemented AI for routine financial tasks. Within the first year, they saved **$750,000**, reduced reconciliation errors by **80%**, and freed up their controllers to focus on strategic initiatives.

The Future of AI in Financial Operations

As you implement AI to optimize routine processes, remember that this is just the beginning. The true potential of AI lies in its ability to evolve alongside your organization. As machine learning models improve and new technologies emerge, controllers can harness even greater efficiencies, insights, and strategic capabilities.

The question isn't whether to implement AI—it's how soon you can start. By embracing these innovations today, you'll position yourself and your organization for success in 2025 and beyond. So, what's your next step? It's time to lead the charge and redefine what operational excellence looks like in the modern era.

Process	Key Metrics Pre-AI	Post-AI Impact	Efficiency Gains	Financial Savings	Examples
Reconciliations	- 40 hours/week spent manually - 20% error rate	- Time reduced by 85% - Error rate reduced by 67%	85% faster	$250,000 annually	Retail company saved $500,000/year in reconciliation processes.
Financial Reporting	- 12 days for quarterly reports - 5% error rate	- Time reduced to 5 days - Real-time reporting added	40% faster	Savings depend on enhanced strategic decisions	Manufacturing firm reduced quarterly reporting by 58%.
Internal Audits	- Duration: 2 months - Fraud detection: Limited	- Audit time reduced by 50% - Fraud detection ↑ 60%	50% faster	Identified $2 million in previously undetected fraud	Financial services firm accelerated audits significantly.
Overall Impact	- Routine tasks dominate time	- Shift to strategic focus - Proactive risk management	Time reallocated to strategic activities	ROI achieved in 12–24 months	Companies reported enhanced compliance and decision-making.

CHAPTER 3: STRATEGIC DECISION-MAKING WITH AI: FROM DATA TO ACTIONABLE INSIGHTS

Imagine this scenario: You're in a boardroom, the CEO is asking for recommendations on where to allocate the next quarter's budget, and every executive is looking at you for clarity. The stakes are high, and the numbers on your dashboard are overwhelming—sales trends, cash flow projections, and economic forecasts, all presented in real-time. What would you do? How do you make decisions that not only justify the company's trust in you but also secure its financial future?

In 2025, controllers and financial leaders are no longer merely gatekeepers of numbers; they are expected to be strategic decision-makers. But here's the challenge: traditional methods of analysis often fall short in handling the complexity and speed of today's business environment. This is where Artificial Intelligence (AI) steps in—not as a replacement for your expertise but as a powerful ally. Have you ever considered how leveraging AI can transform the way you make decisions, turning raw data into actionable insights? Let's explore.

The Growing Complexity of Financial Decisions

As a controller, your role is more demanding than ever before. Global supply chain disruptions, fluctuating interest rates, and the rapid adoption of new technologies have created an environment where static financial models are no longer sufficient. The question is, how can you navigate this complexity without succumbing to analysis paralysis?

AI provides an answer. With tools capable of processing vast amounts of data at lightning speed, AI can identify patterns, correlations, and anomalies that would take a human analyst weeks—or even months—to uncover. For example, imagine a predictive model that not only forecasts revenue but also identifies the specific factors—seasonality, customer behavior, or external economic indicators—driving those numbers. How would that level of granularity impact your strategic planning?

But here's the catch: AI is not a magic wand. While it excels at identifying trends, the real power lies in your ability to interpret those insights and align them with the company's goals. Have you developed the skill set to bridge this gap between raw data and actionable strategy? If not, you're leaving potential value on the table.

From Data Overload to Clear Decision Paths

Be honest—how often do you feel overwhelmed by the sheer volume of data at your fingertips? Cash flow statements, expense reports, market analysis, and operational KPIs are just a fraction of what you juggle daily. Yet, having more data doesn't necessarily mean better decisions. In fact, it often leads to confusion and hesitation. So, how do you cut through the noise?

AI tools like machine learning algorithms and natural language processing can help prioritize what truly matters. For instance, sentiment analysis powered by AI can assess customer feedback across thousands of reviews and social media posts to identify emerging risks or opportunities. Meanwhile, anomaly detection algorithms can flag unusual expenses or deviations in financial trends, enabling you to act swiftly.

Think about this: What if you had an AI-powered dashboard that not only aggregated all your financial metrics but also provided you with scenario-based recommendations? Instead of sifting through hundreds of reports, you could focus on evaluating two or three clear courses of action. How much time—and how many headaches—would that save you?

But here's the critical question: Do you trust these recommendations enough to act on them? Building trust in AI begins with understanding how these systems generate insights. As a financial leader, it's your responsibility to validate the data and ensure it aligns with the company's strategic objectives. This interplay between human intuition and machine precision is where the magic happens.

The Role of AI in Risk Management

Let's consider one of the most nerve-wracking aspects of your role: managing risk. Whether it's protecting the company from fraudulent transactions, forecasting the impact of an economic downturn, or ensuring compliance with ever-evolving regulations, the stakes couldn't be higher. The cost of a wrong decision can be devastating. So, how can AI help mitigate these risks?

AI excels at predictive analytics, offering insights that go beyond traditional risk management tools. For instance, AI can analyze historical data and external factors to predict potential cash flow issues months before they occur. Machine learning models can also detect subtle patterns in transactions that may indicate fraud, often before a human auditor would notice.

Relying solely on AI introduces its own risks. What happens if the algorithms are biased or the data used to train them is incomplete? This is why your role as a controller is indispensable. You must combine the insights provided by AI with your professional judgment and ethical considerations. Have you thought about how to create a governance framework that ensures AI tools are used responsibly and effectively?

Turning Insights into Strategic Actions

Now let's shift gears. Insights are meaningless unless they lead to action. So, the real challenge isn't just gathering data or even analyzing it—it's translating those insights into decisions that drive business success. How do you ensure that your recommendations resonate with stakeholders and lead to measurable results?

One approach is to leverage AI for scenario planning. Let's say you're advising on whether to expand into a new market. An AI-powered tool could generate multiple scenarios, factoring in variables like currency exchange rates, competitor strategies, and local economic conditions. Armed with this information, you could present a data-backed plan that outlines the risks and rewards of each option.

But here's the key: Your ability to communicate these insights clearly and persuasively is just as important as the analysis itself. Have you mastered the art of storytelling with data? AI can provide the foundation, but it's your narrative that will inspire confidence and drive action among your peers and superiors.

Challenges and Ethical Considerations

Before we wrap up, let's address a critical point: AI is not without its challenges. How do you ensure that your reliance on AI doesn't lead to over-automation, where human judgment is sidelined? And what about ethical concerns, such as data privacy or the potential for algorithmic bias?

These are not hypothetical questions. As a controller, you are uniquely positioned to advocate for responsible AI practices. This means asking tough questions: Where is the data coming from? How transparent are the algorithms? Are the insights generated by AI aligned with the company's values and objectives? By taking an active role in these discussions, you can ensure that AI serves as a tool for empowerment rather than a source of risk.

The Future of Decision-Making in Finance

As you look ahead to the challenges and opportunities of 2025 and beyond, one thing is clear: AI is reshaping the landscape of financial decision-making. The question is not whether you will use AI, but how effectively you will integrate it into your role.

Picture yourself five years from now, leading strategic initiatives with confidence because you've mastered the art of combining AI insights with human intuition. What would that version of you look like? How much more impactful would your decisions be?

The journey starts now. By embracing AI as a partner, refining your decision-making skills, and addressing the ethical challenges head-on, you can position yourself as an indispensable leader in your organization. The tools are at your disposal—are you ready to take the leap?

Using Predictive and Analytical Models to Enhance Strategic Planning and Decision-Making

Think about this: What if you could anticipate your company's financial challenges and opportunities six months before they materialize? What if you had the ability to pivot strategies based on trends that haven't yet reached your competitors' radar? These aren't hypotheticals; they're the realities of organizations that effectively utilize predictive and analytical models. Are you among them, or are you still relying on outdated, reactive methods?

Predictive analytics, powered by artificial intelligence (AI), is revolutionizing strategic planning. By leveraging historical data, statistical algorithms, and machine learning, companies can forecast future outcomes with remarkable accuracy. Yet, as with any tool, its effectiveness depends on how well it is implemented and interpreted. In this chapter, we'll explore real-world examples of organizations successfully using predictive and analytical models to improve decision-making and how you can adopt similar strategies in your role.

Predictive Models in Action: Real-World Applications

Let's start with a well-known example: Netflix. The streaming giant doesn't just predict which shows you'll enjoy watching; it uses predictive models for virtually every strategic decision, from content creation to subscriber retention. Netflix analyzes viewing patterns, time of engagement, and customer feedback to determine what kinds of content will resonate with specific audiences. Using these insights, the company allocates its multi-billion-dollar content budget with laser precision.

Now imagine applying this principle to financial planning in your company. Instead of relying solely on traditional budgeting methods, you could use predictive analytics to forecast revenue fluctuations based on external factors like market trends or internal variables such as past performance. How would this change your approach to allocating resources?

Another example is Walmart. During Hurricane Sandy in 2012, Walmart's predictive analytics team noticed an unusual spike in sales of strawberry Pop-Tarts and beer in areas affected by hurricanes. This insight wasn't just a fun fact—it enabled Walmart to optimize its supply chain, ensuring that these items were well-stocked in stores along the storm's path. This kind of actionable insight isn't limited to retail; similar strategies can be applied to inventory management, cash flow optimization, or even workforce planning in your organization.

Enhancing Strategic Planning with Scenario Analysis

Predictive models excel at answering "what if" questions, making them invaluable for scenario planning. Let's break this down with a concrete example.

Imagine you're a financial controller for a mid-sized manufacturing company. Your CEO is considering expanding operations into a new international market. You're tasked with presenting a plan that evaluates the financial viability of this expansion. Traditional methods would involve compiling data on costs, potential revenues, and risks—but this approach is inherently static. It assumes that the current market conditions will remain unchanged, which we know is rarely the case.

With predictive analytics, you can create dynamic scenarios. For instance, a machine learning model could analyze historical sales data from similar markets, incorporating

external factors like currency exchange rates, political stability, and regional economic trends. The model could then generate multiple forecasts:
1. A best-case scenario where revenues exceed projections due to favorable market conditions.
2. A worst-case scenario where geopolitical tensions reduce consumer demand.
3. A most-likely scenario based on current trends and averages.

Armed with this information, you can present the CEO with a nuanced plan that includes actionable steps for mitigating risks (e.g., hedging against currency fluctuations) and maximizing opportunities (e.g., targeting underserved customer segments). How much more compelling would your recommendations be with this level of precision?

Case Study: Predicting and Managing Cash Flow

One of the most critical aspects of your role as a controller is managing cash flow. Inadequate cash flow can cripple even the most profitable companies. Let's look at how General Electric (GE) used predictive analytics to tackle this issue.

In 2018, GE faced significant cash flow challenges. To address this, the company implemented predictive models to analyze its accounts receivable, accounts payable, and inventory turnover. The insights revealed inefficiencies in payment collection cycles and inventory management that were draining cash reserves.

By addressing these specific pain points, GE was able to free up millions of dollars in working capital. What's more, the predictive models didn't just solve the immediate problem—they provided ongoing visibility into potential future cash flow bottlenecks. This allowed the company to proactively adjust its strategies, ensuring long-term financial stability.

Could your company benefit from a similar approach? Imagine deploying a model that forecasts cash flow shortages months in advance, giving you ample time to secure financing, adjust spending, or renegotiate terms with suppliers. The question isn't whether you should implement predictive models for cash flow management—it's how soon you can start.

Bridging the Gap Between Analytics and Action

Despite its transformative potential, predictive analytics is only as effective as the decisions it informs. So how do you ensure that insights from these models translate into strategic actions?

Take the example of Target. The retail giant uses predictive models to anticipate customer needs, famously identifying life-changing events like pregnancies based on subtle changes in purchasing behavior. But Target doesn't stop at prediction; it integrates these insights into its marketing strategy, sending personalized offers to customers at the right time.

This integration is key. In your role, you could use predictive models to identify potential cost overruns in a major project and then work with operational leaders to implement corrective actions before they escalate. Or, you could forecast market downturns and collaborate with the leadership team to diversify revenue streams proactively. The goal is to embed predictive insights into the organization's broader decision-making framework, ensuring they lead to tangible results.

Overcoming Challenges in Predictive Analytics Implementation

No technology is without its challenges, and predictive analytics is no exception. Common pitfalls include poor data quality, lack of expertise, and resistance to change. So, how do you overcome these obstacles?

1. **Invest in Data Quality:** Predictive models are only as good as the data they're built on. This means ensuring that your data is accurate, up-to-date, and representative of the variables you're trying to analyze. For example, a financial services firm might clean and standardize its transaction data before implementing a fraud detection model.
2. **Build Cross-Functional Expertise:** Predictive analytics requires collaboration between financial professionals and data scientists. Do you have the right mix of skills on your team? If not, consider investing in training programs or hiring specialists who can bridge this gap.
3. **Foster a Culture of Trust:** Resistance to predictive analytics often stems from fear—fear of job displacement or distrust in algorithmic decision-making. Address these concerns by involving stakeholders early in the process and demonstrating the value of predictive insights through small, low-risk projects.

A Vision for the Future: Predictive Analytics in 2025 and Beyond

As we approach 2025, the role of predictive analytics in strategic planning will only grow. Advanced AI models will become more accessible, enabling even small and mid-sized companies to leverage their power. But with this accessibility comes responsibility. How will you ensure that your organization uses these tools ethically and effectively?

Picture yourself leading a quarterly strategy meeting. Instead of poring over static reports, you're presenting dynamic forecasts powered by real-time data. You're not just reacting to market changes—you're anticipating them. You're not just identifying problems—you're proposing solutions.

This is the future of strategic decision-making. The question is: Are you ready to embrace it? Predictive analytics isn't just a tool; it's a mindset—a commitment to leveraging data, technology, and expertise to drive better outcomes. Will you take the leap?

CHAPTER 4: OVERCOMING CHALLENGES: ETHICS, DATA INTEGRITY, AND CHANGE MANAGEMENT

As financial controllers embrace artificial intelligence (AI) in 2025, the opportunities are immense, but so are the challenges. To truly thrive in this transformative era, controllers must navigate a labyrinth of ethical dilemmas, ensure unyielding data integrity, and master the art of change management. These interconnected challenges are not just technical hurdles but strategic imperatives that require a blend of innovation, foresight, and resilience.

Ethics in AI-Driven Financial Management

The integration of AI into financial processes introduces ethical challenges that extend far beyond compliance. In 2025, AI systems are no longer limited to predictive analytics or routine automation; they actively participate in decision-making. This new role raises questions about transparency, accountability, and fairness. Controllers must grapple with ensuring that AI models do not perpetuate or amplify biases, whether intentional or unconscious.

For instance, AI algorithms used in credit risk assessment might inadvertently disadvantage certain demographics due to biased training data. Financial controllers, as custodians of organizational integrity, bear the responsibility of scrutinizing these models. They must work closely with data scientists to validate the inputs, monitor outputs, and ensure that decisions align with ethical principles. This includes advocating for diverse datasets and promoting explainability in AI—making sure that models' decisions are understandable and justifiable.

Furthermore, the ethical use of AI demands a commitment to transparency. Stakeholders, from investors to regulatory bodies, expect clarity about how decisions are made. Controllers must bridge the gap between technical complexity and stakeholder understanding, effectively communicating the role of AI in financial outcomes. This level of transparency not only builds trust but also fortifies the organization against potential reputational risks.

Another critical aspect is addressing the "human factor." While AI can streamline processes, it must not replace the human touch in decision-making. Controllers need to strike a balance, leveraging AI for efficiency while retaining human oversight to ensure ethical standards are upheld. This balance is particularly vital when managing sensitive financial scenarios, such as budgeting cuts or resource allocation, where empathy and judgment play a crucial role.

Safeguarding Data Integrity in the AI Era

In the world of AI-powered financial management, data is the lifeblood of the system. However, the reliance on vast amounts of data introduces significant risks related to accuracy, security, and governance. Controllers must ensure that data integrity remains sacrosanct—because faulty or manipulated data can lead to disastrous outcomes.

One of the primary challenges is data validation. In an AI ecosystem, data flows in real time from multiple sources, including IoT devices, transactional systems, and external APIs. Ensuring the accuracy and consistency of this data requires robust validation frameworks. Controllers must implement stringent checks and balances to identify anomalies, detect errors, and prevent data corruption.

Equally important is safeguarding data from cyber threats. In 2025, the sophistication of cyberattacks has reached unprecedented levels, targeting AI systems that process sensitive financial information. Controllers must collaborate with IT and cybersecurity teams to establish resilient defenses. This includes encrypting data, deploying intrusion detection systems, and conducting regular penetration tests to uncover vulnerabilities.

However, data integrity is not just about protection; it's also about governance. Controllers must champion a culture of data stewardship within the organization. This involves defining clear ownership, establishing data access protocols, and fostering cross-departmental collaboration to eliminate silos. The aim is to create a unified data framework that supports accurate analysis and informed decision-making.

Moreover, as regulatory requirements evolve, financial controllers must ensure compliance with data protection laws. Whether it's GDPR in Europe or emerging AI-specific regulations, staying ahead of legal mandates is non-negotiable. Controllers should invest in legal expertise and technology solutions that facilitate compliance, from automated reporting tools to AI auditing software.

Mastering Change Management in an AI-Driven Workplace

The integration of AI into financial management is as much a cultural transformation as it is a technological one. Change management, therefore, emerges as a critical skill for financial controllers aiming to thrive in 2025. Resistance to change, fear of job displacement, and a lack of understanding about AI's potential can hinder adoption and impact organizational performance.

Controllers must begin by fostering a culture of trust and openness. This involves engaging stakeholders at all levels, from C-suite executives to frontline employees, in meaningful conversations about AI's role and benefits. Clear communication is key to dispelling misconceptions and addressing fears. For instance, rather than framing AI as a tool for workforce reduction, controllers should emphasize its capacity to augment human capabilities, enabling teams to focus on strategic tasks.

Training and upskilling are equally crucial. As AI reshapes financial workflows, employees need new competencies to thrive in this environment. Controllers should champion initiatives that equip their teams with the necessary technical and analytical skills. This might include partnering with learning platforms, organizing workshops, or creating internal knowledge-sharing forums. By investing in talent development, controllers not only enhance their teams' proficiency but also build morale and confidence.

Another essential component of change management is aligning AI initiatives with organizational goals. Controllers must demonstrate how AI investments directly contribute to the company's strategic objectives, whether it's improving financial forecasting accuracy, reducing operational costs, or enhancing compliance. This alignment ensures buy-in from senior leadership and secures the resources needed for successful implementation.

Additionally, controllers must remain vigilant about the potential unintended consequences of AI adoption. For example, while automation may improve efficiency, it can also lead to over-reliance on technology. Controllers should establish contingency plans to address system failures, ensuring that manual processes can be temporarily reinstated if needed. This proactive approach not only mitigates risks but also reinforces confidence in AI systems.

Finally, the pace of technological change requires controllers to adopt an agile mindset. Traditional, rigid approaches to change management are no longer sufficient. Instead, controllers should embrace iterative processes, continuously evaluating and refining AI strategies based on feedback and emerging trends. This agility enables organizations to stay competitive in an ever-evolving landscape.

Thriving in the AI Era: A Holistic Approach

Ethics, data integrity, and change management are not isolated challenges; they are interwoven threads in the fabric of AI-powered financial control. To thrive in 2025, controllers must adopt a holistic approach that addresses these challenges collectively. This requires cultivating a mindset of continuous learning, collaboration, and adaptability.

By prioritizing ethical considerations, controllers can position themselves as trusted leaders in the organization, navigating complex dilemmas with integrity and transparency. Through a relentless focus on data integrity, they can ensure the reliability of AI systems, safeguarding the organization's financial health and reputation. And by mastering change management, controllers can drive successful AI adoption, fostering a culture of innovation and resilience.

In the rapidly evolving world of 2025, financial controllers are not just gatekeepers of numbers; they are strategic enablers of growth and transformation. By overcoming these challenges, they can unlock the full potential of AI, setting a new standard for excellence in financial management.

Addressing Ethical Dilemmas, Data Risks, and Leading AI Adoption in Financial Teams

The incorporation of AI into financial management introduces profound shifts, requiring financial controllers to navigate uncharted waters. To harness its transformative power, leaders must address ethical dilemmas, manage data risks, and guide their teams through the adoption process. These challenges are not just technical or operational—they are deeply human and strategic. With the global AI market in finance projected to reach $37.9

billion by 2027, growing at a CAGR of 26.6% from 2022 , controllers must act decisively to ensure sustainable success.

Ethical Dilemmas in AI-Powered Finance

Ethical dilemmas in AI stem from its ability to influence decision-making, resource allocation, and risk assessments in ways that are not always transparent. For instance, consider the use of AI in predicting fraud. While AI can flag transactions for review, false positives disproportionately targeting specific demographics raise questions about fairness. In 2025, companies deploying AI face not only operational challenges but also reputational risks if such biases are left unaddressed.

Financial controllers can address these issues by implementing ethical guidelines tailored to AI operations. For example, Deloitte recommends developing an AI ethics framework that includes fairness, transparency, and accountability as core principles . Controllers should also champion the creation of cross-functional ethics committees to oversee AI initiatives and resolve dilemmas proactively.

One striking example is a major European bank that leveraged AI to optimize its loan approval process. While the system increased approval speed by 40%, it inadvertently denied a higher percentage of loans to applicants from low-income neighborhoods due to historical biases in its training data. To rectify this, the bank's financial controller led a review of the algorithm, retrained it using a more diverse dataset, and instituted mandatory bias testing. This not only improved equity in decisions but also enhanced customer trust.

Controllers must also navigate ethical concerns about the role of human oversight in AI-driven processes. As AI increasingly automates tasks, the question of accountability arises. For example, if an AI system makes an error in financial forecasting, who is responsible— the developer, the operator, or the financial controller? The answer lies in establishing clear accountability protocols, where controllers ensure human oversight remains integral to all AI-driven decisions.

Data Risks in AI Systems

Data lies at the heart of AI's functionality, but it also presents significant risks. A 2023 survey revealed that 68% of finance professionals considered data quality as their primary AI implementation challenge . Poor data quality can lead to inaccurate insights, financial mismanagement, and even regulatory violations. Controllers must therefore prioritize rigorous data governance practices.

1. Data Bias

Bias is a pervasive risk in AI systems, stemming from training datasets that reflect historical inequities or incomplete information. For example, a multinational corporation deploying AI to assess investment risks found that its system undervalued renewable energy projects due to insufficient representation of such ventures in its dataset. To combat bias, controllers must ensure datasets are diverse, representative, and continuously updated to reflect evolving realities.

2. Data Security
Cybersecurity threats are another pressing concern. In 2024, a leading financial firm experienced a breach where hackers manipulated AI training data, causing incorrect risk assessments that cost the firm $15 million in losses. To prevent such scenarios, controllers should work with IT teams to implement advanced security measures such as data encryption, real-time anomaly detection, and blockchain for audit trails.

3. Data Compliance
Regulatory compliance adds another layer of complexity. With AI-specific regulations, such as the EU's AI Act, mandating strict standards for transparency and accountability, financial controllers must adopt proactive compliance strategies. This includes conducting regular audits, maintaining clear documentation of AI processes, and deploying AI tools designed to monitor adherence to regulatory frameworks.

A notable case is a U.S.-based insurance company that faced penalties for violating GDPR due to inadequate data anonymization in its AI models. To address this, the company's controller implemented automated compliance checks, reducing future risk and positioning the organization as a leader in ethical data usage.

Leading AI Adoption in Financial Teams

The adoption of AI in financial teams requires effective leadership to overcome resistance, build capabilities, and align initiatives with organizational goals. Research shows that 52% of employees in financial services express anxiety about AI replacing their roles, underscoring the need for controllers to manage change empathetically .

1. Building Awareness and Trust
Controllers must begin by fostering awareness and trust within their teams. A large global bank, for instance, launched a series of workshops where controllers and data scientists demystified AI's role in financial processes. These sessions highlighted AI's potential to enhance, rather than replace, human expertise. As a result, employee engagement improved, and resistance to AI initiatives declined by 35%.

2. Upskilling the Workforce
AI adoption demands new skills, including data analytics, model interpretation, and AI system management. Financial controllers can lead upskilling efforts by investing in targeted training programs. For example, a mid-sized enterprise that introduced AI for cash flow forecasting partnered with an online learning platform to train its finance team in Python and machine learning basics. The result was a 20% increase in forecasting accuracy and greater employee confidence in using AI tools.

3. Piloting AI Initiatives
Controllers should start small, piloting AI initiatives in specific areas to demonstrate value and refine implementation strategies. A retail company tested AI-powered expense management software in one department before scaling it company-wide. This phased approach allowed the controller to gather feedback, address concerns, and adjust workflows, ensuring a smoother transition.

4. Promoting Collaboration
AI adoption is most successful when it is a collaborative effort. Controllers should act as bridges between finance, IT, and other departments, ensuring alignment of goals and resources. A pharmaceutical firm's controller led a task force comprising finance, IT, and HR teams to integrate AI into budgeting processes. By involving stakeholders early, the project achieved a 95% adoption rate within the first year.

5. Continuous Evaluation and Iteration
Finally, controllers must embrace an iterative approach to AI adoption. This involves continuously evaluating AI systems' performance, gathering user feedback, and making adjustments as needed. A logistics company using AI for expense reporting discovered inefficiencies in its initial deployment. By incorporating employee suggestions and fine-tuning the system, the company reduced processing times by 50%.

The Role of Financial Controllers in AI-Driven Transformation

In 2025, the role of financial controllers has evolved beyond managing numbers—they are strategic leaders at the forefront of AI-driven transformation. By addressing ethical dilemmas, safeguarding data, and leading their teams effectively, controllers can unlock AI's full potential. The stakes are high, but so are the rewards: organizations that successfully implement AI in finance report a 38% improvement in decision-making speed and a 27% reduction in operational costs on average .

As AI continues to reshape the financial landscape, controllers who embrace these challenges with foresight and determination will not only drive organizational success but also set new benchmarks for ethical, data-driven leadership in the digital age.

Category	Key Insights	Statistics/Examples
Ethical Dilemmas	AI introduces fairness, transparency, and accountability challenges.	- 40% faster loan approvals, but bias against low-income applicants in European bank case.
	Accountability in AI decisions is critical.	- Ethics frameworks recommended by Deloitte; human oversight essential.
Data Risks	Poor data quality impacts insights, compliance, and decisions.	- 68% of finance professionals cite data quality as their main AI challenge (2023 survey).
	Bias in datasets skews outcomes.	- AI undervalued renewable energy projects due to historical biases in data.
	Cybersecurity threats require robust defenses.	- A $15M loss from manipulated AI training data in a 2024 financial firm case.
	Regulatory compliance is non-negotiable.	- GDPR violation by U.S. insurance firm led to penalties; fixed via automated compliance checks.
Leading AI Adoption	Employee anxiety about AI must be addressed.	- 52% of finance employees express job replacement fears (2024 survey).
	Upskilling workforce enhances AI adoption.	- Mid-sized company improved cash flow forecasting by 20% through Python and ML training.
	Piloting AI projects reduces implementation risks.	- Retail firm improved workflows with department-level AI testing before scaling.
	Collaboration ensures smooth adoption.	- Pharmaceutical firm achieved 95% adoption rate with cross-department AI task force.
	Continuous evaluation optimizes performance.	- Logistics firm reduced expense reporting times by 50% after iterative improvements.
Overall Impact	AI enhances decision-making and reduces costs.	- 38% improvement in decision speed and 27% reduction in operational costs for successful adopters.

CHAPTER 5: THE CONTROLLER OF THE FUTURE: SKILLS, MINDSETS, AND LEADERSHIP IN AN AI WORLD

In a rapidly evolving financial landscape, the role of the financial controller is undergoing a profound transformation. Artificial intelligence (AI) is no longer a distant concept but a tangible reality reshaping corporate finance. By 2025, controllers will need to adopt a proactive stance, developing not only technical expertise but also strategic vision, emotional intelligence, and leadership skills. This chapter delves into the essential competencies and mindsets for the controller of the future, offering actionable insights and real-world examples to equip financial professionals to thrive in an AI-driven world.

1. From Data Managers to Strategic Leaders

Traditionally, financial controllers have been seen as gatekeepers of data accuracy and compliance. Their primary focus has been on closing books, ensuring regulatory adherence, and providing historical financial reports. However, AI has automated many of these routine tasks. By 2025, up to 70% of transactional accounting processes are expected to be automated, according to a Deloitte survey. This shift demands a redefinition of the controller's role—from data managers to strategic advisors.

Controllers must now interpret AI-driven insights, guide decision-making, and collaborate with cross-functional teams. For example, AI can forecast cash flows with a 90% accuracy rate based on historical and real-time data, but it requires a human touch to align these forecasts with broader business strategies. This evolving role necessitates enhanced analytical skills, creativity, and a deep understanding of the organization's objectives.

2. Essential Skills for the AI-Powered Controller

a. Digital Literacy and AI Proficiency

By 2025, financial controllers must master AI tools and platforms such as robotic process automation (RPA), predictive analytics, and natural language processing (NLP). A McKinsey report highlights that 83% of finance functions in leading organizations are already using or planning to implement AI solutions. Controllers must understand how these tools work, their limitations, and how to leverage them effectively.

For instance, using NLP algorithms, controllers can automate the extraction of insights from unstructured data such as emails, contracts, and invoices. This not only reduces manual effort but also enhances data-driven decision-making.

b. Strategic Thinking and Business Acumen

AI can provide insights, but it cannot replace strategic judgment. Controllers must hone their ability to connect financial data with operational metrics, market trends, and organizational goals. This skill enables them to provide actionable recommendations rather than just reporting numbers.

c. Leadership and Change Management

The integration of AI in finance often encounters resistance due to fears of job displacement and complexity. Controllers must become change leaders, advocating for the adoption of AI and guiding their teams through this transition. They must communicate the benefits of automation while fostering a culture of continuous learning.

d. Emotional Intelligence and Collaboration

Despite the rise of AI, human interaction remains critical. Controllers must exhibit high emotional intelligence (EQ) to manage stakeholder relationships, resolve conflicts, and build trust. Their ability to collaborate across departments, bridging the gap between finance, operations, and technology, will be a key differentiator.

3. Mindsets for Success in an AI-Driven World

a. Growth Mindset

As technology evolves, so must the mindset of financial controllers. A growth mindset—embracing challenges, persisting through setbacks, and viewing failure as a learning opportunity—is essential. Controllers must stay curious, continuously upskilling themselves in emerging technologies and methodologies.

b. Adaptability and Agility

The pace of change in AI and technology is relentless. Controllers need to remain flexible, adapting quickly to new tools, regulations, and business models. Agility also involves embracing experimentation, testing new AI solutions, and iterating based on feedback.

c. Ethical Responsibility

AI brings ethical challenges, including data privacy, bias in algorithms, and transparency issues. Controllers must ensure that AI implementations adhere to ethical standards, fostering trust among stakeholders. For example, in 2023, several financial institutions faced scrutiny due to biased credit-scoring algorithms, highlighting the need for ethical oversight.

d. Future-Oriented Vision

Controllers must anticipate future trends, such as the impact of quantum computing on encryption or the integration of blockchain in finance. By staying ahead of the curve, they can position their organizations for long-term success.

4. Case Studies: Controllers Thriving in the AI Era

Case Study 1: A Multinational Adopts Predictive Analytics

A global manufacturing company implemented AI-powered predictive analytics to streamline inventory management. The controller spearheaded this initiative, aligning AI outputs with the company's operational goals. The result? A 25% reduction in inventory costs and a 15% improvement in cash flow forecasting accuracy. By leveraging AI insights, the controller demonstrated how finance can drive operational excellence.

Case Study 2: Building a Culture of Innovation

At a mid-sized tech firm, the financial controller introduced RPA to automate invoice processing, saving the finance team over 1,000 hours annually. Recognizing fears of job loss, the controller organized workshops to upskill employees, focusing on strategic analysis and client engagement. This approach not only improved efficiency but also boosted team morale and engagement.

5. Metrics That Matter in 2025

As controllers transition to strategic roles, the metrics they prioritize will evolve. Instead of focusing solely on historical financial indicators, they will track forward-looking, AI-enabled KPIs such as:

- **Predictive Cash Flow Accuracy**: How closely AI-generated forecasts align with actual outcomes.
- **Return on AI Investment (RoAI)**: The financial impact of AI implementations relative to their cost.
- **Process Automation Rate**: The percentage of finance processes automated using AI.
- **Team Productivity Metrics**: Time saved and value-added activities performed post-AI adoption.

According to Gartner, organizations with high AI adoption rates see up to a 20% increase in finance team productivity and a 10% reduction in operational costs.

6. Challenges and Opportunities Ahead

Challenges

While AI offers immense potential, it is not without challenges. Common obstacles include:
1. **Data Quality Issues**: AI models require high-quality data to function effectively. Inconsistent or incomplete data can lead to inaccurate outputs.
2. **Resistance to Change**: Employees may fear job displacement or struggle to adapt to new technologies.
3. **Regulatory Complexity**: AI adoption must comply with evolving regulations, particularly regarding data privacy and security.

Opportunities

Despite these challenges, AI opens unprecedented opportunities for controllers to add value:
1. **Enhanced Forecasting**: AI enables real-time forecasting, allowing organizations to respond proactively to market changes.
2. **Strategic Partnering**: Controllers can leverage AI insights to collaborate with CEOs, CIOs, and other leaders on growth initiatives.
3. **Cost Optimization**: Automation reduces operational costs, freeing up resources for strategic investments.

7. Preparing for the Future: A Roadmap

To succeed in 2025 and beyond, financial controllers should follow this roadmap:

1. **Invest in Continuous Learning**: Stay updated on AI advancements through courses, certifications, and industry events.
2. **Build a Tech-Savvy Team**: Recruit and upskill team members in AI and data analytics.
3. **Embrace Collaboration**: Partner with IT and operations teams to ensure seamless AI integration.
4. **Prioritize Ethics and Governance**: Establish clear guidelines for AI usage, focusing on transparency and accountability.
5.

The controller of the future is not merely a financial steward but a strategic leader who bridges the gap between technology and business strategy. By mastering AI tools, adopting a growth mindset, and prioritizing collaboration and ethics, controllers can position themselves as indispensable assets in an AI-driven world. The journey is challenging, but for those who embrace change, the opportunities are limitless.

Key Skills and Mindsets to Excel as a Financial Leader in an AI-Driven Environment

As artificial intelligence (AI) reshapes industries, financial leaders must adapt to a world where success hinges not only on technical prowess but also on strategic insight, emotional intelligence, and ethical responsibility. This shift requires an evolution in both skills and mindset. The financial leader of tomorrow must combine digital fluency with a people-first approach, harnessing AI to drive innovation while safeguarding organizational integrity. This section explores the essential capabilities and mindsets for financial leaders to thrive in an AI-powered environment, illustrated with real-world examples and supported by compelling statistics.

1. The Technical Proficiency Imperative

AI's integration into finance has transformed how organizations approach tasks like budgeting, forecasting, and risk management. For instance, AI-powered platforms can analyze vast datasets in seconds, detecting patterns that would elude even the most seasoned analyst. By 2025, it is estimated that 85% of finance tasks will be augmented by AI, according to a PwC report. This reality underscores the need for financial leaders to develop a robust technical foundation.

a. Mastery of AI Tools and Platforms

Financial leaders must understand how AI technologies function and their potential applications. Tools such as robotic process automation (RPA), machine learning algorithms, and predictive analytics are becoming indispensable. For example, BlackLine's AI-powered reconciliation software has reduced manual efforts by up to 70% for global companies, enabling teams to focus on strategic initiatives.

b. Data-Driven Decision-Making

AI thrives on data, and financial leaders must become adept at interpreting its outputs. This involves not only analyzing AI-generated insights but also questioning their validity. In one case study, a multinational firm using AI for credit risk assessment found that 12% of its models exhibited bias due to flawed training data. The financial leader's role was pivotal in identifying and rectifying these biases, ensuring ethical outcomes.

c. Continuous Learning in Technology

With advancements in AI occurring at a rapid pace, financial leaders must commit to lifelong learning. Platforms like Coursera and edX offer specialized courses on AI in finance, providing an accessible way to stay ahead. A survey by LinkedIn Learning found that 78% of finance executives who invested in tech-focused education saw measurable improvements in team performance within six months.

2. Strategic Vision and Innovation

AI may automate processes, but strategic thinking remains uniquely human. Financial leaders must cultivate the ability to see the big picture, aligning AI initiatives with organizational goals to unlock transformative value.

a. Scenario Planning and AI Forecasting

AI excels in predictive modeling, but its forecasts must be contextualized within broader strategic frameworks. For instance, an AI model predicting a downturn in demand might suggest budget cuts, but a financial leader might balance this with long-term investment in innovation. In 2023, Amazon demonstrated this approach by leveraging AI to anticipate holiday sales fluctuations while simultaneously investing in robotics to enhance warehouse efficiency—a decision that boosted operational capacity by 25%.

b. Encouraging a Culture of Innovation

Financial leaders play a critical role in fostering an innovative mindset within their teams. By 2025, organizations prioritizing innovation are expected to outperform peers by 2.5 times in revenue growth, according to Gartner. Financial leaders can champion hackathons, cross-departmental projects, and AI-driven pilots to encourage experimentation and creative problem-solving.

3. Emotional Intelligence (EQ): The Human Factor in AI Leadership

While AI handles technical tasks, the interpersonal dimension of leadership cannot be replicated. Emotional intelligence (EQ) is increasingly recognized as a cornerstone of effective financial leadership.

a. Building Trust in AI Integration

The adoption of AI often generates apprehension among employees, who fear job displacement or loss of control. Financial leaders must address these concerns through empathetic communication and transparent decision-making. For example, a Fortune 500 company implementing AI-based fraud detection conducted town hall meetings led by its CFO, highlighting how AI would reduce repetitive tasks while creating opportunities for employee growth. This approach resulted in a 30% increase in employee satisfaction scores.

b. Collaborative Leadership

Cross-functional collaboration is critical in an AI-driven environment, as financial leaders must work closely with IT, marketing, and operations teams. A high EQ enables leaders to navigate these interactions effectively, balancing competing priorities and fostering a shared vision. The introduction of AI-powered dashboards at a leading retail chain, for instance, succeeded largely due to the CFO's ability to bridge gaps between data scientists and store managers, ensuring the tool addressed real-world challenges.

c. Managing Conflict with Finesse

AI implementations often spark debates over resource allocation and strategic priorities. Financial leaders must mediate these conflicts, using empathy and negotiation skills to align stakeholders. An example from the energy sector involved a CFO resolving tensions between R&D and compliance teams over AI investment, resulting in a balanced approach that achieved regulatory compliance while fostering innovation.

4. Ethical Leadership in an AI World

As AI becomes central to financial decision-making, ethical considerations take on heightened importance. Financial leaders must ensure that AI applications uphold transparency, fairness, and accountability.

a. Safeguarding Against Bias

AI systems are only as unbiased as the data they are trained on. A Harvard study found that 57% of AI models used in finance exhibited some form of bias, often disadvantaging certain demographic groups. Financial leaders must establish robust governance frameworks, auditing AI models regularly to mitigate such risks.

b. Promoting Data Privacy

Data is the lifeblood of AI, but its use must comply with privacy regulations like GDPR and CCPA. Financial leaders are responsible for ensuring that AI deployments respect customer and employee data rights. In one notable example, a global bank faced a $50 million fine in 2022 for non-compliance with data privacy laws—a cautionary tale emphasizing the importance of ethical oversight.

c. Establishing Ethical AI Policies

To build trust, financial leaders should formalize ethical AI policies that address issues such as algorithmic transparency and accountability. For instance, Microsoft's Responsible AI framework serves as a benchmark, offering guidelines on ethical AI usage that can inspire similar initiatives within the financial sector.

5. The Resilient Mindset: Thriving Amidst Uncertainty

In an era defined by rapid change, resilience is a vital attribute for financial leaders. This mindset enables them to navigate disruptions with confidence and poise.

a. Learning from Failure

AI implementations often involve trial and error. Financial leaders must embrace failures as learning opportunities, iterating and refining approaches. For example, a fintech startup that initially struggled with AI-powered credit scoring adjusted its algorithm based on feedback from rejected applicants, ultimately increasing loan approvals by 15% without compromising risk.

b. Staying Agile in Crisis

Whether facing economic downturns, regulatory shifts, or cybersecurity threats, financial leaders must remain agile. AI can provide real-time insights to guide decision-making, but leaders must interpret these insights within the context of broader market dynamics. During the COVID-19 pandemic, companies with agile financial leadership were 40% more likely to maintain profitability, according to Bain & Company.

c. Cultivating Optimism

A positive outlook is essential for inspiring teams and driving long-term success. Financial leaders who frame AI as an enabler of growth rather than a threat foster a culture of optimism, empowering employees to embrace change. A healthcare provider that framed its AI rollout as a step toward improving patient care saw 95% of its staff support the initiative.

6. Examples of Financial Leadership Excellence in the AI Era

Case Study 1: Transforming Treasury Operations

A multinational corporation implemented AI-driven treasury management tools to optimize cash flow. The CFO led this transformation, using AI to predict currency fluctuations with 88% accuracy and automating 60% of treasury tasks. The result was a 12% reduction in transaction costs and a significant improvement in liquidity management.

Case Study 2: Enhancing Fraud Detection

In the insurance industry, a CFO collaborated with IT teams to deploy AI-based fraud detection algorithms, identifying fraudulent claims with a 95% accuracy rate. This initiative saved the company $8 million in the first year, demonstrating the value of strategic AI investments.

Case Study 3: Building an AI-Ready Workforce

At a tech startup, the CFO championed an upskilling initiative, offering courses on AI and data analytics to all finance employees. This investment resulted in a 30% increase in efficiency and positioned the company as an industry leader in financial innovation.

7. Measuring Leadership Success in an AI Environment

To assess the effectiveness of financial leadership in an AI-driven world, organizations can track the following metrics:

- **AI Adoption Rate**: Percentage of finance processes automated or augmented by AI.
- **Ethics Compliance Score**: Evaluation of adherence to ethical AI guidelines.
- **Employee Engagement Metrics**: Indicators of team morale and satisfaction post-AI integration.
- **Financial Impact**: ROI from AI investments, measured through cost savings and revenue growth.

The rise of AI has ushered in a new era for financial leaders, redefining their roles and responsibilities. To excel in this environment, leaders must combine technical expertise with strategic vision, emotional intelligence, and ethical accountability. By embracing continuous learning, fostering innovation, and prioritizing transparency, financial leaders can not only adapt to change but also drive their organizations toward unparalleled success in an AI-driven world. With the right skills and mindset, they can transform challenges into opportunities, ensuring their legacy as pioneers of the AI era.

APPENDICES

Appendix A: Case Studies in AI-Driven Financial Control

AI technology has revolutionized financial control, providing organizations with the tools to optimize processes, enhance accuracy, and drive strategic decision-making. Below are real-world case studies of companies that successfully implemented AI in their financial departments, showcasing tangible benefits and transformative outcomes.

Case Study 1: A Multinational Retailer's Journey to Real-Time Expense Management
A leading global retailer struggled with delayed financial reporting and inaccuracies in expense tracking across its regional operations. Implementing an AI-powered expense management system revolutionized their approach. Using machine learning algorithms, the system automatically categorized expenses, identified anomalies in real-time, and provided predictive insights into spending trends.

As a result, the company reduced manual processing time by 60%, decreased reporting errors by 75%, and improved decision-making by enabling real-time visibility into financial data. Furthermore, AI-driven analytics empowered regional managers to identify cost-saving opportunities, such as optimizing procurement practices and renegotiating vendor contracts.

Case Study 2: AI-Powered Forecasting in a Manufacturing Firm
A medium-sized manufacturing company faced challenges in predicting cash flow due to fluctuating demand and supply chain complexities. By adopting an AI-based forecasting platform, the company gained the ability to analyze historical financial data alongside external factors such as market trends and raw material prices.

The AI system provided highly accurate cash flow forecasts, which enabled the finance team to plan inventory purchases more effectively and reduce excess stock by 20%. Additionally, the improved forecasts allowed the company to secure more favorable financing terms with banks, boosting liquidity and operational efficiency.

Case Study 3: Automating Compliance for a Financial Services Provider
A financial services firm operating in multiple jurisdictions faced rising compliance costs due to stringent regulations and frequent audits. Incorporating an AI-driven compliance solution streamlined their processes by automating regulatory reporting, monitoring transactions for potential breaches, and ensuring timely filings.

The implementation led to a 40% reduction in compliance-related expenses and minimized the risk of fines associated with non-compliance. Additionally, the AI solution identified areas where operational adjustments could improve adherence to new regulatory requirements, positioning the company as a market leader in ethical financial practices.

Case Study 4: Enhancing Decision Support at a Healthcare Organization
A large healthcare provider needed better tools to manage its complex financial structure, which included numerous cost centers, billing systems, and payment models. AI-powered analytics tools transformed their financial decision-making by integrating disparate data sources and presenting actionable insights through intuitive dashboards.

With AI, the organization identified inefficiencies in billing processes and optimized resource allocation, resulting in annual savings of over $5 million. AI models also highlighted patterns of delayed payments, prompting the finance team to improve collection strategies, which reduced outstanding receivables by 30%.

Case Study 5: AI-Driven Fraud Detection at a Tech Startup
A fast-growing tech startup experienced significant vulnerabilities in its financial processes due to rapid scaling and limited internal controls. By deploying an AI-powered fraud detection system, the company enhanced its ability to identify and mitigate risks. The system analyzed transactions, flagged suspicious activities, and provided insights into fraudulent behavior trends.

Within the first year, the startup prevented over $250,000 in potential losses due to fraud and strengthened stakeholder confidence by demonstrating its commitment to financial integrity. Additionally, the insights from the AI system helped refine their internal controls, ensuring long-term financial stability.

Appendix B: AI Tools and Platforms for Financial Controllers

As AI adoption accelerates, financial controllers have access to an ever-expanding array of tools and platforms designed to streamline operations, enhance accuracy, and drive value. Below is a curated list of essential AI tools and platforms, categorized by their primary use cases.

1. Financial Planning and Analysis (FP&A)
- **Anaplan**: A cloud-based platform offering predictive analytics and scenario planning. AI-powered models help financial controllers forecast revenue, expenses, and cash flow with precision.
- **Adaptive Insights**: Specializes in budgeting and forecasting, leveraging machine learning to analyze trends and provide actionable insights.

2. Expense Management
- **Expensify**: An AI-driven tool that automates expense tracking and reporting. Its OCR (Optical Character Recognition) capabilities extract data from receipts, categorizing expenses and flagging anomalies.
- **Concur**: A comprehensive platform integrating AI to manage travel and expense workflows, offering fraud detection and policy compliance features.

3. Accounts Payable (AP) and Receivable (AR)
- **Tipalti**: An AI-powered AP automation tool that streamlines invoice processing, payment approvals, and global supplier payments.
- **HighRadius**: Specializes in automating AR processes, using AI to optimize credit scoring, collections, and cash application.

4. Fraud Detection and Risk Management
- **Fraud.net**: Combines machine learning and real-time analytics to detect fraudulent activities in financial transactions.

- **SAS Fraud Management**: Offers AI-driven solutions to monitor, detect, and prevent fraudulent activities across financial systems.

5. Compliance and Regulatory Reporting

- **AxiomSL**: Provides AI-powered solutions for regulatory reporting, ensuring accuracy and timeliness while adapting to evolving compliance requirements.
- **ComplyAdvantage**: Uses machine learning to automate regulatory compliance processes and monitor transactions for potential risks.

6. Data Visualization and Business Intelligence

- **Tableau**: While not exclusively AI-based, Tableau integrates AI capabilities to analyze and visualize complex financial data effectively.
- **Microsoft Power BI**: Offers AI-driven analytics tools for financial controllers to uncover trends, create interactive dashboards, and share insights across teams.

7. Forecasting and Predictive Analytics

- **Workday Adaptive Planning**: Uses machine learning algorithms to create accurate forecasts and identify potential financial risks.
- **Alteryx**: Combines data preparation, analytics, and AI modeling to provide insights for predictive financial planning.

8. Payroll and Human Resources Integration

- **Gusto**: An AI-enhanced payroll platform that ensures compliance with tax regulations, simplifies benefits administration, and provides detailed financial reporting.
- **BambooHR**: Offers AI-driven insights into workforce costs, helping financial controllers align HR expenses with overall financial strategies.

9. Treasury and Cash Management

- **Kyriba**: An advanced treasury management system with AI-powered cash forecasting, risk management, and liquidity optimization features.
- **Trovata**: Automates cash management processes by integrating bank data, providing AI-driven cash flow analysis and forecasting.

10. ERP Systems with AI Integration

- **Oracle NetSuite**: A robust ERP platform incorporating AI to optimize financial processes, including reporting, consolidation, and compliance.
- **SAP S/4HANA**: Uses machine learning and predictive analytics to enhance financial reporting and operational efficiency.

Key Considerations When Selecting AI Tools

- **Integration**: Choose tools that seamlessly integrate with existing systems such as ERP or CRM platforms.
- **Scalability**: Ensure the AI tool can grow with your organization and adapt to increasing complexity.
- **Ease of Use**: User-friendly interfaces and intuitive functionalities are critical for driving adoption among finance teams.
- **Customization**: Opt for platforms that allow tailored configurations to align with your organization's specific needs.

Appendix C: Glossary of Key Terms in AI and Financial Control

The rapidly evolving field of AI-driven financial control introduces a host of technical terms and concepts that financial controllers must understand to effectively leverage these technologies. Below is a glossary of key terms to facilitate comprehension:

- **Artificial Intelligence (AI)**: A branch of computer science focused on creating systems capable of performing tasks that typically require human intelligence, such as learning, reasoning, and problem-solving.
- **Machine Learning (ML)**: A subset of AI where algorithms learn and improve from data without being explicitly programmed. Commonly used for forecasting, fraud detection, and process automation.
- **Robotic Process Automation (RPA)**: Technology that automates repetitive tasks by mimicking human actions in digital systems. Useful in accounts payable, invoicing, and compliance reporting.
- **Predictive Analytics**: Techniques leveraging historical data to predict future outcomes, aiding in budgeting, risk assessment, and cash flow forecasting.
- **Natural Language Processing (NLP)**: A field of AI that enables machines to understand and interpret human language. Common applications include automating financial document reviews and generating reports.
- **Neural Networks**: A framework inspired by the human brain, used in deep learning to identify patterns and relationships in complex datasets.
- **API (Application Programming Interface)**: A set of rules that allows software programs to communicate, crucial for integrating AI tools with existing financial systems.

This glossary provides a foundational understanding, enabling financial professionals to navigate and communicate effectively within the AI landscape.

Appendix D: Checklist for Implementing AI in Financial Operations

Adopting AI in financial operations can be transformative, but it requires careful planning and execution. This checklist outlines a practical, step-by-step guide to ensure successful integration:

1. **Assess Organizational Needs**:
   - Identify pain points in financial processes (e.g., inefficiencies, errors, compliance issues).
   - Define clear objectives for AI implementation, such as improving accuracy or reducing costs.
2. **Evaluate Current Systems**:
   - Conduct an audit of existing financial tools and processes to determine compatibility with AI solutions.
   - Assess data quality and accessibility, as clean, structured data is critical for AI success.
3. **Research AI Solutions**:
   - Explore tools tailored to financial operations, such as predictive analytics platforms or RPA software.
   - Compare features, costs, scalability, and user reviews to select the best fit.
4. **Engage Stakeholders**:
   - Collaborate with finance teams, IT staff, and leadership to align expectations and secure buy-in.
   - Address concerns about change management and provide training as needed.
5. **Pilot and Test**:
   - Launch a pilot project in a specific financial area (e.g., accounts payable automation).
   - Monitor performance metrics and gather user feedback to refine the implementation.
6. **Roll Out and Monitor**:
   - Gradually expand AI usage across departments while ensuring continuous support.
   - Regularly review outcomes, update systems, and address challenges to optimize performance.

This checklist equips financial controllers with a structured approach to integrate AI, ensuring maximum efficiency and impact.

Appendix E: Resources for Continuous Learning in AI and Finance

Staying current in AI and finance is essential for professionals aiming to thrive in a technology-driven landscape. Below are curated resources to support continuous learning:

Books

- *Prediction Machines: The Simple Economics of Artificial Intelligence* by Ajay Agrawal, Joshua Gans, and Avi Goldfarb – A foundational guide to understanding the economic implications of AI.
- *Financial Analytics with R* by Mark J. Bennett and Dirk L. Hugen – A practical resource on applying analytics to financial datasets.

Online Courses

- *AI for Everyone* (Coursera): A beginner-friendly introduction to AI concepts and their business applications, offered by Andrew Ng.
- *Machine Learning for Finance* (Udemy): Focused on using machine learning to solve financial problems, with real-world examples.

Webinars and Podcasts

- *AI in Finance Webinar Series* (MIT Sloan School of Management): Regular sessions on cutting-edge AI applications in finance.
- *FinTech Insider Podcast*: Covers AI, innovation, and trends in financial technology.

Communities and Forums

- *LinkedIn Groups*: Join professional groups like "AI in Finance" to connect with industry peers.
- *Kaggle*: A data science community offering competitions, datasets, and learning opportunities in AI.

These resources provide financial controllers with knowledge, skills, and networking opportunities to remain at the forefront of AI advancements.

END

www.ingramcontent.com/pod-product-compliance
Lightning Source LLC
Chambersburg PA
CBHW070938220526
45469CB00007B/2439